# Her Special Vision

*Contemporary Canadian Biographies*

# Her Special Vision

## A Biography of Jean Little

### By Barbara Greenwood and Audrey McKim

*Series Editor: Gladys E. Neale*

**IRWIN PUBLISHING**
Toronto, Canada

Copyright © 1987 by Irwin Publishing Inc.

ISBN 0-7725-1664-2

Canadian Cataloguing in Publication Data
Greenwood, Barbara, 1940-
Her special vision

(Contemporary Canadian biographies)

ISBN 0-7725-1664-2

1. Little, Jean, 1932- . 2. Novelists, Canadian
(English) - 20th century - Biography.* 3. Blind -
Canada - Biography. I. McKim, Audrey, 1909- .
II. Title. III. Series.

PS8523.I87Z72 1987     C813'.54     C87-094369-3
PR9199.3.L57Z72 1987

Design by Artplus/Brant Cowie
Typeset by Compeer Typographic Services Limited
Printed and bound in Canada by Imprimerie Gagné Ltée

Published by

Irwin Publishing Inc.
180 West Beaver Creek Road
Richmond Hill, Ontario
L4B 1B4

Cover Photo: Jean and Missy in Judy Coulman's class at Edward Johnson
Public School in Guelph
(Jean Little Collection)

1 2 3 4 5 IG 91 90 89 88 87

# Contents

ACKNOWLEDGMENTS

The authors wish to thank Dr. Flora Little, Jean and the family for their co-operation in supplying information, recollections and photographs for this biography.

The excerpt on page 50 is taken from the poem "A Friendship Is a Fragile Thing", found in *Take Wing*. Copyright © 1968 by Jean Little. Reprinted by permission of Little, Brown and Company.

The excerpt on page 69 is taken from the poem "For My Father", found in *When the Pie Was Opened*. Copyright © 1968 by Jean Little. Reprinted by permission of Little, Brown and Company.

# Introducing Jean

Jean sits facing the class, her round face alight with fun as she nears the end of the story she's telling. At her feet a golden labrador retriever slumbers, eyes blinking open occasionally as the audience of ten-year-olds murmurs or giggles. Jean pauses — a professional storyteller holding her audience. Then comes the punchline. "After a while it dawned on me that I didn't have a cut on my knee. All morning I sat with my right leg crossed over my left knee. After lunch, I came back to school with bandaids plastered on both knees. And that's how I got out of putting my name on the board."

The audience collapses in laughter at the unexpected ending to this reminiscence from Jean's childhood. The golden labrador's head swings up, and he looks around at the children in seeming approval. His Jean has done it again. He settles down for another few minutes of peace while Jean answers questions: "Where do your ideas come from? Is it hard to write a book? Do you make much money? Do you use a typewriter?" Then one child blurts out, "How can you type when you're blind?"

(Jean Little Collection)
*Jean and Zephyr at Edward Johnson Public School, Guelph*

Jean Little, one of Canada's most popular authors of children's books, answers all their questions. She wants children to know what a writing life is really like. Even more, she wants them to understand that handicaps may be overcome or compensated for in different ways.

# CHAPTER 1

# Family
# Beginnings

Jean's story begins with an indomitable grandmother. As a young bride Margaret Gauld travelled with her husband William to the Orient. Grandfather Gauld died before Jean was born but she loved to hear stories about how her grandparents met and set out on their great adventure.

"Your grandfather grew up on a farm near London, Ontario," Grandma Gauld told her. "He worked hard at university with the idea of becoming a missionary. I was visiting friends in Saskatchewan when I first met him. He was a student minister working in a country parish for the summer. One day he got lost on his visiting rounds and ended up at my friend's gate. Soon I was helping him in his church services by playing the organ and leading in the hymn singing."

When Jean's grandparents were married they went to live in Taiwan under the missionary board of the Presbyterian Church. William Gauld was to spend half his life on the island. His main interest was in teaching and preaching, but much of his time was spent planning and supervising the building of schools, hospitals, colleges and houses.

To "break ground" for the buildings was not a simple matter. Many Chinese of that time were superstitious. They believed the land was ruled by spirits of wind and water. The spirits would be angry if the earth were disturbed by foreigners. They were also afraid that the foreign seeds planted would produce strange vegetables which might poison the people. Margaret planted cabbages in her garden against Chinese wishes. Many years later she was given credit for introducing one of the island's most popular vegetables. The cabbage has now become a mainstay of the Taiwanese diet.

After William died in 1923, his wife became a missionary in her own right. She taught music in the church and college so successfully that the Presbyterian Church in Taiwan is considered a "singing church" to this day and Margaret Gauld is remembered as Chit-nng-san-si or 1-2-3-4, a nickname given her by her students who liked to tease her affectionately about the 1,2,3,4, beat of her baton.

Jean's mother, Flora, spent the first five years of her life in Taiwan playing with Chinese children and learning their language as quickly as she did her own. When she was old enough for school, her mother took Flora and her two sisters home to Canada. They lived in Ontario with Mrs. Gauld's parents and Flora's two older brothers. When Flora's mother and younger sister went back to Taiwan, nine-year-old Flora and her older sister went to live with an aunt and uncle in Regina, Saskatchewan. Flora was sixteen before her parents came home on furlough and the family was reunited.

Flora had always wanted to be a nurse but by the time she was old enough to go to university that ambition had changed. Instead she became a doctor and, at medical school, she met Llewelyn Little. Llew had an appealing personality and a deep sense of purpose. Flora, with her family background in church work, was interested to learn that he had applied for missionary work overseas.

To be accepted as a missionary, Llew had to submit testimonials regarding his character from people who knew him well. These tributes are still on file in the archives of the United Church. Among the interesting things said about him back in 1923 is a quote from George A. Little (no relation), Editor of *Presbyterian Publications*:

> He has a sense of humour. No one appreciated the humour of the situation more than Llew when he went out to address a congregation in Northern Ontario, driving fourteen miles with a slow horse in a storm and found a congregation of one — a deaf mute.
>
> Incidentally, he had prayers with the man and wrote him a Christian message to carry home that will be long prized.
>
> Llew's father was an inimitable mimic and his son inherits the gift. At one time I feared that he might use his fun-making gift for ridicule in a way that might give pain. I have no fear on this score now. He has as much fun in him as ever, but it is tempered by charity and sympathy and kept under perfect control.

After graduating from medical school, Flora returned to Taiwan to work under the Presbyterian Foreign Mission Committee. Llew had to stay in Canada. He had not yet graduated and also he felt responsible for the welfare of his widowed mother and younger sisters. Once his sisters were able to earn their own living, Llew was free to marry.

In 1927 Flora returned to Canada to marry Llew. Years later Jean would ask, "Why do we always have pork and beans on your wedding anniversary? Other people have lovely dinners."

"Pork and beans WAS our wedding supper," her parents explained, laughing at the memory.

(Jean Little Collection)
*Flora and Llew in 1924, before they were married*

Flora and Llew had decided they would marry in Toronto before going on to Llew's family in Guelph. Because Flora had recently arrived in Canada, they didn't have time to have the banns read in church. Dr. George Pidgeon, then minister of Bloor Street United Church, helped them get a special licence allowing them to be married the same day.

The family in Guelph prepared a big supper in anticipation of their homecoming. When they didn't arrive, another dinner was prepared the next night. The third night Llew's sister said, "If they arrive tonight, it will be pork and beans." And, of course, that was the very night they arrived.

Four years later the English Presbyterian Church offered Llew the position of medical missionary in Tainan, a city in southern Taiwan. So Flora with her husband and young son, Jamie, returned to the land of her birth.

In 1931, Taiwan was controlled by the Japanese. They had modernized the island and improved the educational system so that every child attended school.

"For us it was much like living in Canada," Flora recalls, "as far as electricity and other modern conveniences were concerned. The mission compound where we lived had a seven-foot high brick wall with a gate between it and the main road. Inside were four very solid, brick houses which my father had built. Three of the houses were for married missionaries and the other, for unmarried missionary women. My mother and my unmarried sister, Gretta, lived in one of these houses.

"The hospital was in the compound, too. The Chinese people came in, to the hospital. Some of them lived across the street from the compound in one-storey houses with mud floors.

"The rainy season came in February and March. Their houses were flooded whereas ours were built up high and were not, so they all came over and slept on our floors. The first floor of the house was crowded with people who stayed until the flood was over. Then they went back to clean up the mess."

Flora was not a staff doctor in the hospital because much of her time was spent caring for her growing family: Jamie, at first, and then Jean, Hugh, and Patricia. Instead, she acted as her husband's interpreter while he served his patients. She was also the unofficial social worker and backup person that every missionary needs.

Both Jean's mother and her grandmother could have held their heads high in the feminist movement of today. They had fulfilling and useful careers at a time when it was very unusual for women to work outside the home. Their drive and determination was passed on to Jean.

# CHAPTER 2

# Jean
# in Taiwan

On January 2, 1932 Flora Jean Little was born — blind.

When Flora and Llew realized there was something wrong with their baby's eyes, they took her to a Japanese eye specialist in Tainan. He found that Jean had corneal scars which almost covered the pupils of both her eyes. He recommended special drops to dilate the pupils.

As the days went by, Jean's parents found that she began to turn to the light. The drops seemed to be working. Then the baby experienced an allergic reaction and the drops had to be discontinued. Even without the drops, Jean continued to turn to the light. This gave her parents hope — she was not completely blind.

Flora never forgot the joy and excitement she felt when one-year-old Jean reached out for a spoon. She had actually seen something and wanted to hold it!

When Jean was three, her parents took a short furlough to Canada. There, they took her to another eye specialist, but the verdict was the same. Her sight would improve as long as her eyes were growing. Soon she would be able to see out from around the scars. What the doctors couldn't predict was how much sight she would eventually have.

(Jean Little Collection)
*Tainan, October 1932. Llew and Flora Little with Jamie and six-months-old Jean*

Jean's vision did improve, but beyond a few feet the world remained blurred and indistinct. Both parents were determined that she would be treated like a normal child. They had no patience with the attitudes of some friends and relatives who wanted to say: "Poor child. Let me do that for you." Llew and Flora felt that love, not pity, was what Jean needed. Even when her blindness created problems that made them long to keep her safe at home, they hid their fears and treated her just like their other children. So well did they succeed that for the first five years of her life Jean didn't know she was handicapped.

Stumbling, falling, and bumping into things didn't prevent her from tagging after her older brother, Jamie, and the other children in the mission compound. They all played together—mission children who lived behind the walls and the Taiwanese children who came in each day with their mothers and fathers who worked as cooks and nursery helpers. Jean and Jamie spoke the Amoy dialect as easily as they spoke English, so the whole group played happily in the enclosed garden. Jean joined in every game and helped to act out the stories Jamie liked to dramatize.

Jean's first clue that she was different from other children came from Marilyn Dickson, a girl a year younger than Jean who lived in another of the mission houses. One day Jean and Marilyn were playing in the garden. Marilyn was perched high on a branch of the banyan tree.

"You can't climb up here," she called as Jean started up.

"I can so." Jean struggled up to the next branch.

"No, you can't. My mother says you have bad eyes and I have to take care of you and make sure you don't do anything dangerous."

Jean was indignant. "That's not true! *My* mother never said anything like that. I'm going to ask her."

They ran into the house and confronted Flora.

"You do have poor eyes, Jean," she said, "but you can go right ahead and climb that tree if you want."

Jean's mother was amused to see the two children face each other triumphantly and shout, "See!"

Jean soon found an area in which her poor sight caused her frustration and stress. She had always loved listening to stories but by the time she was five she wanted to read them for herself just the way Jamie did. He would lose himself in books for hours but she could see only a grey blur when she looked over his shoulder. Flora had taught Jamie to read from the family's collection of books. For Jean, she ordered special books from Canada. The words were printed in large black type. The learning process would be difficult but Jean's mother tackled it with enthusiasm and originality.

Using a printing set with letters an inch high, Flora printed Jean's first reading lessons on a large chart. Jean could not see the whole chart at once. Because she had to look out from around the scars covering her pupils she could only see large objects in sections. When she looked at a tree she would see the bottom first, then the middle, then the top. Only if the tree were very small and far away could she see the whole of it at once. To compensate for that problem her mother propped the chart on a stand and Jean walked back and forth in front of it seeing a few words at a time.

There were other problems, too. Each eye focussed at a different point. If she tried to use both eyes to read, her left eye would cross over and make the print look blurred. She soon learned to use only one eye at a time, squinting down the line of print with her right eye in which the vision was much better. When her eyes got tired the muscles jerked so that the letters seemed to be dancing on the page.

Reading was a slow process, but Jean didn't mind. She loved the smell and feel of books as much as the wonderful stories on their pages. Through them, her

(Jean Little Collection)
*Jean at 5 with Hugh and Jamie (in his school uniform)*

inner world of imagination grew rapidly. One story in particular caught her interest — her brother Jamie's favorite, *Robin Hood*. Jamie often organized the children of the missionary compound into players to act it out. Jean longed to be Maid Marion but Jamie had decreed that Maid Marion had curly golden hair. Therefore Marilyn Dickson was always chosen to play that part. Jean was more suited to play roly poly Friar Tuck.

One day Marilyn was away. At last Jean had her opportunity. She threw herself into the part she knew so well, imagining herself the perfect Maid Marion. Near the end of the story, as Jamie was carrying her across "a rushing stream in Sherwood Forest" (really a ditch of water in the rice paddies behind the compound), he dropped her and she came back to reality — soaking wet.

On Easter Sunday of the year Jean turned six, her sister Patricia was born. Hugh and Jean had known for some months that their mother was going to have a baby. Jean had been told it would be a live doll for her. If it were a boy his name would be Patrick, if a girl, Patricia. Either way the baby would be called Pat.

That Sunday, Jean and Hugh had been sent to visit a neighbour. Jamie was away at school. Jean remembers they were sitting in the living room listening to an Easter story being read aloud when she saw her grandmother's head go past the window. Grandma was very excited, and told them their father wanted them to come home at once. They ran as fast as they could go.

Llew met them in the hall and said, ''Guess who's upstairs.''

''Mother?''

''Who else?''

Hugh and Jean puzzled over that for a moment. Who else could be upstairs? Suddenly they remembered. ''Pat?'' they said together.

''That's right.'' Father took them upstairs. There, in Aunt Gretta's arms, wrapped in a yellow and white blanket, was a crying baby. Jean wanted to take her real live doll in her own arms, but Aunt Gretta wasn't about to let a six-year-old hold a newborn baby. Jean discovered right away that this live doll was not going to be all hers!

Not long after Pat was born, Llew's term as missionary in Taiwan came to an end. The Littles moved to Hong Kong where Llew was to take the place of a doctor who was on leave.

# CHAPTER 3

# A Widening World

For Jean, the move to Hong Kong brought new challenges. In Taiwan, Flora had taught Jean to read and spell but she wanted to see how Jean would fit into a regular school. Their short stay in Hong Kong coupled with the small classes at a nearby school seemed the ideal opportunity.

Right from the beginning, however, there were problems. The teacher found she couldn't give Jean as much time as the child needed. For the first, but not the last, time in her life, Jean found playing games with other children frustrating and humiliating. She remembers sitting in a circle of children for a game of "Drop the Handkerchief." Suddenly everybody began shouting at her to run. Jean jumped up in confusion. She had no idea the hanky had been dropped behind her, and she couldn't see well enough to know where to run so she ran to her mother. Flora turned her daughter around, told her to be a good sport, and sent her back. Jean felt betrayed.

Trying to cartwheel was another frustration. It looked so easy, but Jean always fell sideways. Why couldn't she flip over as the others did, she was always asking.

School was a trial for Jean, but family life made up for it. She remembers her father teaching her to swim.

(Jean Little Collection)
*Llew and Flora Little with Grandma Gauld, Aunt Gretta, Hugh, Jamie, Jean and baby Patricia in 1938*

It wasn't the lessons she loved so much as the safe, secure feeling she had when she clung with her arms around his neck as he swam.

Jean's great need to have an important place in the family surfaced when she was very young. She and Hugh, her younger brother, were friends but they were rivals, too. One day, Llew decided to test Hugh's will power. Hugh had been gorging on a favourite type of cookie. His father put a plateful of the cookies on the dining-room table and stood Hugh in front of them saying, "Now, if you have willpower, you can stand and look at those cookies without taking any. See how long you can do that!"

Jean wanted to be tested, too, but her father said no, this was a special test for Hugh. When Llew left, Jean began to tease Hugh to take a cookie but he stood there staring at the full plate with his hands firmly linked behind his back. Llew was busy and forgot about the test. After what must have seemed hours to a small boy, his father returned to find Hugh still staring at the cookies. He scooped the boy up in a big hug and told him how wonderful his willpower was.

Jean was quite jealous, but she felt better when she remembered a story about herself and her father that she had heard over and over again. A visitor had come to the house soon after Jean was born. Embarrassed and confused by the baby's blindness the guest blurted out, "Isn't it too bad that she isn't a boy to be friends with Jamie."

Llew, holding the baby in his arms, said proudly, "I wouldn't trade Jean for a million boys."

Jean treasured that story as much as she treasured the memories of sitting on her father's lap, showing him the pictures she had drawn. Even when his children were very small Llew gave them helpful hints

(Jean Little Collection)
*Hugh, Jean, and Jamie in Hong Kong*

about how to improve what they were trying to do. Jean showed him her drawing of Hugh using a hose in the garden. "Hugh should be bigger than the hose," her father pointed out but he added, "In all your pictures, Jean, your people are alive and that's what really matters. They're alive!"

Jean's ability to make people and situations come alive on paper and in her imagination occasionally made life difficult for her as she grew up. An incident occurred in Hong Kong which would trouble her for many years. Every day she and Hugh walked back and forth to school together. One day, a friend of their father's offered them a ride home. Jamie, who was home from boarding school, saw them get out of the car. He was horrified when he discovered they didn't even know the man's name.

"He might have been a kidnapper," he exclaimed. "Do you know what kidnappers do? They put gags on your mouth and take you to their home and tie you to a chair. Then they send a letter to your mother and father asking for money. If they won't send money, the kidnappers saw off your foot and send it in a parcel. When your parents get the parcel it says: Send money or we'll saw off her other foot. If you go getting in people's cars that'll happen to you."

That grisly story was to surface in Jean's mind some years later.

The Littles' stay in Hong Kong was short. Llew was convinced that war was coming. He wanted his wife and children safe. Flora felt sure people could not be so stupid as to start another world-wide conflict just twenty years after the war that was supposed to end all wars. Besides she was reluctant to leave her husband who had another six months to work before his contract with the hospital expired.

Flora, however, didn't like some aspects of life in Hong Kong. Her children couldn't play with the Chinese children as they had in Taiwan. The medical community lived around the hospital, near the top of the mountain. The Chinese people not only lived too far down the mountain for Jean and Hugh to visit easily, they also spoke a different dialect than Jean spoke. Flora was afraid her children would inadvertently learn intolerance, so, when the headmistress of Jean's school told her that the teacher couldn't give Jean the individual attention the child needed, there was no further question about what to do. They must go back to Canada and enroll Jean in a sight-saving class.

Llew bought the tickets and put his family on the boat for Canada — just in time. It was August, 1939. War was declared in September.

# CHAPTER 4

# Home
## to Canada

Jean and her brothers asked endless questions about Canada, that faraway world their parents called home. Although most of their storybooks were about British or American children, in Jean's mind they all showed pictures of "home." Hugh and Jean had their own ideas of what Canada was all about. For five-year-old Hugh, it was Mounties. He had his own red Mountie jacket and wide-brimmed hat but he wanted to see a real Canadian Mountie.

To Jean, Canada meant snow. She longed to see it, feel it, and roll in it. One birthday, her mother made a snowball from a large Japanese paper ball wrapped in cotton wool. Inside she tucked small presents, each with a string attached. The ball sat in the centre of the table until the end of the party when the children pulled the strings, tearing it apart. That had been fun, but it wasn't the real thing. Now they were going home to Canada — home to snow, and Mounties, and an extra surprise for Jean. A letter from Canada told her Aunt Ruth, her father's sister, would have a new doll waiting for her when she arrived.

Only snatches of the journey back to Canada impressed themselves on Jean's seven-year-old mind. She remembers that her mother and brothers were seasick

(Jean Little Collection)
*Hugh in his Mountie uniform*

and she was not. When she bragged about this later to her father he was amused and told her he was never seasick either.

"It's the shape of our heads, Jean. If you have a long head you get seasick. If you have a square head like ours, you don't. Square heads are the best kind to have!"

After the ship came the train. The long ride from Vancouver to Toronto is hazy in Jean's mind but she vividly remembers the day they looked out the train window and saw a Mountie on the platform in Regina. Hugh's wish had been granted.

The travellers were welcomed with affection and relief by members of the family in Ontario. Aunt Ruth had the promised doll waiting there for Jean — a large baby doll Jean called Susan. Jean still has her today.

Susan was all that Jean had hoped for. She became a well-loved companion and the focus of many childhood memories. One day, several years after Jean had received Susan, three-year-old Pat threw the doll out of the window. The whole top of Susan's head came off. Jean went crying into the house with the broken doll. But her father knew what to do. He took Susan into his office for an examination telling Jean to sit in the waiting room just like any distraught parent. Finally, he brought the doll back with her head all taped up.

"I've operated on her, Jean, and she'll be fine now," he said as he put Susan into his daughter's arms.

"I cared about her so much," recalls Jean, "I wouldn't even leave her downstairs at night. I was afraid of the dark and I was sure she was too. I remember lying in bed thinking: She's just a doll. She's not afraid of the dark. Then I'd think: How do I know that? And I'd get up and go get her to take her to bed with me.

"One day I went for a walk with Susan all wrapped up in a blanket. A lady coming out of a funeral home said, 'Isn't it beautiful to know that a new life is beginning.' I was so embarrassed. I didn't say a word about Susan's being just a doll."

Susan was a comfort to Jean in the difficult settling-in days in Toronto. When they first arrived, Flora and her children stayed with her mother and sister Gretta, who had previously returned to Toronto. Four children and three adults crowded the tiny apartment so Flora was relieved when she found a house for rent on Kingswood Road. Jean was able to attend Duke of Connaught School with Jamie because it had a sight-saving class. But this time, they had to go to school by streetcar. Jean didn't have any trouble with streetcars while Jamie was with her. She just followed him.

One day, however, he was sick and had to stay home. Jean went off to school alone, confidently following other children who took the streetcar. Coming home was different, however. No other child got off at her

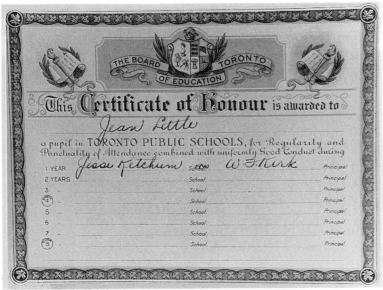

(Jean Little Collection)

*Jean's Attendance Card for Jesse Ketchum Public School in
Toronto*

street. She couldn't see well enough to recognize any landmarks so she just stayed on the car. At the end of the run, she was the only passenger left. The driver finally asked her where she was going. In tears she told him Kingswood Road. An hour later she was back with her panic-stricken family. Until that incident, Jean didn't know how much she depended on Jamie. Flora realized that she would have to anticipate such problems for her young daughter.

In November, the house on Kingswood Road was needed by its owner so the Littles moved to Bedford Road. From there the children could walk to Jesse Ketchum Public School.

The sight-saving class had twenty pupils in various grades. Seven-year-old Jean was put in Grade 2.

The atmosphere of the schoolroom was very much like home to her. The children were free to move about and go right up to the green chalkboard to peer at the writing if they needed to. They were encouraged to discuss their problems and interests. Their work went up on the walls for everyone to see and enjoy.

Jean soon discovered one advantage of a multi-grade classroom. Once she had finished her own work she could listen in on other classes or read their books. She particularly enjoyed *The Third Reader* where she discovered a poem beginning:

> My child, should you decide to go
> And make your home in Mexico,
> The proper place for you to settle
> Is on Mount Popocatepetl.

With her nose smudged by the print from the page, Jean went to the teacher to learn the pronunciation of the last word. She was so delighted with its nonsensical sound that she immediately learned to spell it both forward and backward. After that, when visitors came to the classroom, Miss Bogart would say, ''Now before you leave, Jean will spell Popocateptl backwards.'' Jean would then ''perform,'' basking in the surprise and amusement of the visitors.

Edna Bogart was an imaginative and understanding teacher. She knew that Jean needed encouragement and a feeling of accomplishment. Jean loved Miss Bogart. She remembered that classroom so vividly that years later, when she was writing *From Anna*, she recreated its warm atmosphere and understanding teacher.

The children at Jesse Ketchum Public School came from many backgrounds. Often they dressed up in their national costumes. For one concert, the pupils were to represent dolls from different lands. A teacher pretended to wind each ''doll'' with a key, and then the doll would dance or sing. One girl, whose parents were

(Jean Little Collection)
*Jean learning a Japanese dance while the family was still in Taiwan*

from Czechoslovakia, did a folkdance. Jean was dressed in a kimono . . .

". . . which was wrong for Taiwan — and I was to sing *Jesus Loves Me* in Taiwanese. Well, I got stuck. Suddenly, out of the audience came Mother's voice singing the next line. I was *so* mortified. Everyone else's mother was quiet and well-behaved but my mother had to sing the next line! What could be nicer than a mother who would help you out? But that's not what I thought at the time."

Jean was happy in Grade 2 at Jesse Ketchum but outside the classroom was a harsh world. When Jean tried to make friends in the schoolyard she was shunned. If she persevered the other children pushed or chased her.

One day, she was allowed to take her mother's best umbrella to school. She walked along twirling it proudly. Suddenly a seventh grade boy grabbed it from her, stamped on it and broke its spines. She returned home crying, dragging the umbrella behind her "like a dead bird."

Such unpleasant occurrences happened often. Flora knew her daughter was being harassed because her eyes made her look strange and she attended a special class. It was unfair and unkind but she did not go to the school to report on the children's actions. Jean was a sturdy little girl with an independent will and Flora's wisdom overcame her feelings of protectiveness.

"My mother never made her grief my burden," Jean recalls. "Now I realize she must have felt agony when I was mistreated. I'm glad that she was wise enough not to be overprotective. But at the time I was frustrated and angry. Mother would be very, very sympathetic and would comfort me, but she'd say, 'You have to learn to laugh at it. Pay no attention to it.' " And so, at seven, Jean began the frustrating search for friendship and acceptance that was to last until her teens.

At home, life was much happier. Jean had Hugh and Jamie to play with and at Christmas her father finally arrived. To Jean it seemed ages since she had seen him. Would she know him? The family met him at Union Station in Toronto. Much to Jean's relief she recognized him immediately. They had a wonderful Christmas but sadness lay behind their joy. Soon after Christmas Llew had to return to Japan to take over a doctor's practice in Kobe.

By the time he returned from Japan that summer, the war they had all feared had exploded both in Europe and the Pacific. Llew felt he ought to join the navy now that his own country was at war. But he was turned down because he was over forty and he had four children. (In 1940, Canada still had many young, unmarried men to send into the fighting.) So the Littles moved to Llew's hometown of Guelph. There, the two doctors set up their medical practices together in a large house and the family settled down for a long stay.

# C H A P T E R   5

# The Lonely Time

In November, 1940, Jean started Grade 4 in a Guelph elementary school. So far school life had been a series of disappointments for her. She found the work impossible to copy off the blackboard. She had no friends because her wandering left eye made other children feel uneasy. And, on the way between the safety of the schoolroom and the comfort of home, she was often scared.

"I wasn't too afraid in the schoolyard," Jean remembers, "because there was usually a teacher around, but I was afraid when we left. I would run to get home."

Jean was often followed by a gang of children shouting, "Cross-eyed! Cross-eyed!" Some even threw stones. In the schoolyard she was excluded from games or forced to be the end person in "Crack-the-Whip." She can still recall that stomach-lurching feeling when the whip cracked and sent her staggering blindly down the schoolyard hill.

Playgrounds in those days were divided into girls' sides and boys' sides. One of the most popular activities on the girls' side was skipping double dutch. Though she practised constantly, Jean could not run in without tangling the ropes. Finally she learned to turn double dutch and became an "ever-ender." Always turning and never skipping wasn't much fun, but at least she was allowed to play.

Jean was not a gloomy, despairing child. She couldn't find a real friend, so she retreated into her imagination for fun and friendship. In the schoolyard stood a huge, old tree. Jean would lean against the rough, scratchy trunk at recess and whisper to it. She felt the tree understood.

She also had other ways of dealing with loneliness. The winter she was in Grade 4 she had a pair of white snowboots trimmed with fur.

''The moment I saw them in the store, I guessed there was something special about them. I was right. When I put them on and went outside I was invisible. Nobody could see me! All that winter I walked around the town being invisible. When people came toward me on the sidewalk I would jump out of the way because I was sure, if I didn't, they would walk right into me. Being invisible was exciting and wonderful. The sky looked bigger and bluer. I felt full of power and magic. I even thought, if I ever wanted to, I could fly with those boots on. But I never tried.

When spring came and I had to put my boots away, I started walking home from school backwards. I went carefully every step of the way without ever turning around. I told myself that if I did it just right I would find a surprise waiting when I got home. Maybe a rich uncle, of whom I had never heard, would come home from sailing around the world and bring me a live monkey! That was my favourite idea but I had others too.

I would step along backwards, so carefully, and I would make up names for my monkey and plan where he would sleep. When I got home I would open the big front door with an excited feeling. Day after day nobody different was there, no uncle, no pet monkey.

But that did not spoil it for me. I had much more fun walking home from school than the other girls I knew who always walked frontwards and never imagined things inside their heads." (written for *Surprise*, United Church of Canada, 1974)

Even though it was engrossing, living in her imagination wasn't completely satisfying. Jean wanted a real friend to walk home with. One girl in particular appealed to her. Shirley had long, golden ringlets and had come from England as an evacuee. Europe was at war, and when heavy bombing began in Britain, many parents sent their children to friends and relatives in Canada to keep them safe. Shirley's accent and circumstances made her seem different and interesting. Jean longed to talk to her.

In Grade 5 it happened. Jean and Shirley were put in the same class. To Jean's delight, the teacher asked Shirley to help Jean to find the right line at recess time. Shirley smiled sweetly and said, "Yes, Miss Marr" but the minute they were out of the teacher's sight Shirley hissed, "You stay away from me," and ran off.

Looking back, Jean knows that Shirley had her own problems. Her accent and her background made her different enough without being saddled with someone else who was shunned by the group. But, at the time, Jean was devastated.

That incident confirmed Jean's determination to fit in at any cost.

One day, in September, shortly after her disappointment with Shirley, Jean was walking to school deep in a pleasant daydream when she suddenly realized the streets were quiet. No other children were on their way to school. With a stomach-wrenching pang Jean realized that the bell had rung. She was going to be late. Back in the forties, being "on time" was essential. Latecomers were punished. They could be sent to the office or kept in to do extra work. Jean didn't care so much about that. A worse fear loomed up in her head. Miss Marr, the Grade 5 teacher, made latecomers put their names on the blackboard and stay in after school.

Jean hadn't been in the class very long and she couldn't see the blackboard anyway, so she didn't know whether the other children wrote their whole name, just their initials, or their first names and last initials. She was sure she would do it wrong and at recess there would be more name-calling. "Stupid Jean doesn't know how to put her name on the board!" She could almost hear the jeers as she made her way down the silent hall to the classroom. What could she do? What could she say?

She opened the door. Just as she'd feared, the whole class turned to look at her. "Why are you late?" the teacher demanded.

"Well," Jean began. Then it came to her in a great flood, the perfect excuse. Taking a deep breath she plunged in. "I was getting ready to leave," she began. "I was just going out the door when the phone rang. I went back because I was the only one at home. Both my parents are doctors, you know. I picked up the receiver and said, 'Dr. Little's residence,' and a voice shrieked,

'MY DAUGHTER IS DYING! MY DAUGHTER IS DYING!'

"So I said, 'Well, I'm very sorry to hear that, but if you'll call back in an hour my parents will be back.'

" 'DON'T HANG UP! DON'T HANG UP! My daughter is dying right this minute. Won't you please come and save her life?' I said, 'Well . . . if she's dying . . . I'll be late for school but I suppose I can't do anything else. I'll have to come and save her. Where do you live?'

He told me he lived on King Street. I went to the office, got the right medicine and ran out the front door.

"I didn't go down Norwich Street and across the Norwich Street bridge because that would have taken too long and I was going to be late for school. I went right down the London Road, crossed at the stepping stones, ran up the hill and down King Street."

Jean paused. The teacher stared at her, speechless. Jean took a deep breath and continued.

"They lived in a log cabin with the wind whistling through the cracks. The door was standing open. There were a lot of people inside, all crying. I said, 'What's the matter?' and they said, 'You're too late. She's dead.' I said, 'Can I please see her?'

"They let me see her, and there she was on a trundle bed. Her skin was blue. Her fingers were bent over backwards and her toes were curled. Her eyes had rolled up so only the whites showed and her teeth were clenched.

"I said, 'Oh, she's not dead. She's just nearly dead.' So I knocked her bottom jaw open and poured the medicine in. Her eyes rolled down. She turned a normal colour, batted her eyes and said, 'Where am I?' I didn't wait to answer because I knew I would be late for school.

"I started for the door but before I could get there all the people went down on their knees between me and the door. They held onto my skirt and wouldn't let me go. 'We'll give you anything' they said, 'gold, emeralds, a horse that comes when you whistle. Just tell us what you want more than anything else in the world and you can have it for saving her life.'

"I said, 'All I want is to be on time for school.' So they got out of my way and I ran out the door, down the street, down the hill, across the stepping stones. I was in such a hurry I went too fast and tripped on the stepping stones, fell into the river, cut my knee, had to go home and change my clothes and put a bandaid on my knee. Then I ran all the way to school and that's why I'm late.''

When she finally came to the end of her inventiveness, Jean peered apprehensively at the teacher. Miss Marr's eyes were closed, her expression resigned. She raised one hand and pointed. ''Just — take — your — seat,'' she sighed.

Jean sat down feeling quite pleased with herself until she remembered she had no bandaid on her knee. She spent the rest of the morning trying to keep her knees out of sight, then rushed home at noon to sneak some bandaids from her mother's supply and plaster them over her knees.

But Miss Marr must have understood the loneliness behind Jean's flight into fantasy. She never questioned the story.

Most of Jean's teachers were helpful and sympathetic. Two of them had had polio which had left one with a crippled arm and the other with a severe limp, so they understood Jean's struggle. From an itinerant teacher, they got books with large print and learned ways of helping Jean fit into a regular classroom. Miss Marr, the Grade 5 teacher, taught her to touchtype on a primary typewriter which made it much easier for her to copy notes and write out lessons. The teachers were careful not to make a fuss over Jean, not to give the other children more cause to resent her. Even so, Jean felt like an outcast. She compensated by retreating into her imagination.

# Imagination —
# Lies?

In the magic world inside Jean's head, she became everything she felt she wasn't in real life — beautiful, clever, heroic. Her favourite book at that time was *The Secret Garden* by Frances Hodgson Burnett.

''I liked to read books in which there was a heroine who was basically unhappy and lived in a miserable situation where everything was wrong and then she would change everything around and it would end up all right. In *The Secret Garden*, Mary was a nasty child and then she turned into a nice child. Somehow that gave me a great feeling of hope. I didn't think that consciously but I read over and over books like *Anne of Green Gables*, *Little Lord Fauntleroy*, *Rebecca of Sunnybrook Farm* and dozens more.''

In Grade 5, Jean made the leap from reading about heroic girls and boys to writing about them. She had just finished reading Albert Payson Terhune's dog stories when the urge to write struck. In an orange Jumbo Scribbler, she began a story about ''a little boy who had a collie dog and lived with his mother in a hut on the top of a mountain.''

In the course of the story, boy and dog braved flood, famine, whirlwind, and grizzly bears to bring the doctor to the boy's sick mother. Jean enjoyed writing the story so much that she immediately began another.

Jean's storywriting grew out of her storytelling. She had told herself bedtime stories for years, then shared them with her sister as Pat grew older. Because Pat was six years younger than Jean, she started out as the listener but soon she was contributing her ideas too. Together they made up a whole boarding school full of characters, each sister playing different roles with different voices. Before falling asleep they'd act out another episode in the continuing saga.

Storymaking was the good side of Jean's imagination but there was another side as well. Because she could fantasize an everyday happening into an exciting story it was sometimes tempting to distort an incident until it became a lie.

One day, when she was walking home with her Grade 5 teacher, Jean told Miss Marr about the names the other children called her. At first she stuck strictly to the truth, listing only the names she really had been called, but Miss Marr was so sympathetic that Jean got carried away. All the names that characters in books had been called came back to her. Her list grew longer and longer until she suddenly found herself repeating out loud the exotic names Diamond had been called in George Macdonald's *At the Back of the North Wind*. Not until she added ''God's baby'' to her list did Miss Marr protest. Jean solemnly assured her that she had indeed been called ''God's baby,'' then spent an agonizing few days hoping Miss Marr wouldn't read the book!

''I had tremendous guilt feelings about lying,'' she remembers. ''I would lie in bed at night worrying that one day Mother and Dad would realize what a liar I was. They would be so angry with me and so upset they wouldn't love me anymore. It never really came through to me that they already knew. It never occurred to me that it would be something I would just outgrow.''

Because lying is part of growing up, Jean shows many of the characters in her books struggling with the temptation and the consequences. Janie Chisholm in *One To Grow On* fantasizes to make herself seem more interesting but just earns the scorn of her family and friends. Meg Copeland in *Spring Begins In March* lies to cover up her poor school marks and learns the agony of waiting to be discovered.

Jean's vivid imagination also made her the victim of exaggerated fears. Lightning terrified her. As a small child she would run to her mother and cling until the storm was over, convinced the lightning would kill them. One day, on the way home from school, she ran into a strange house because she couldn't stand to be out in the storm.

By the time she was ten, everyone was fed up with Jean's fears.

''Just ignore her,'' Jean's father told the family. ''She's being ridiculous.'' But he wasn't entirely without sympathy.

One night there was a very bad storm. The blinds on Jean's window flashed white leaving her huddled under the blankets in terror. Suddenly the ceiling light went on and there was her father, walking around the room, talking casually. He never said, ''I know you're frightened,'' but he stayed until the storm calmed.

Jean's parents tried to offer comfort without encouraging Jean to be dominated by her fears. But they were unable to foresee all the situations that could lead to paralyzing fear for an imaginative child — the story of the kidnappers, for example. That should have been a minor incident, forgotten as soon as they left Hong Kong. Instead it tormented Jean for years.

When the family moved to Guelph, Jean spotted a house, on her route to school, that looked just like the kind of house kidnappers would live in.

"It was very tall and sinister-looking. Every time I got to that corner, I would run the whole block to get past. I loved it when the teacher walked with me. I knew she would look after me when we passed the kidnapper's house.

"I thought Mother had never heard of kidnappers because she didn't seem to worry when I went out. One day I said, very casually, 'You know, kidnappers might get me.'

'No kidnapper will ever take you,' Mother said, 'because we don't have any money.'

'Aaagh!' I thought. 'They'll saw off my feet and little bleeding parcels will arrive at our door.' I was scared about that for years."

Jean's mother knew that the lies and exaggerations came from a lively mind. She tried to protect her daughter from the negative results of that inventiveness. "You must make your imagination your servant, not your master," she often pointed out.

Of course no one learns that lesson overnight.

Gradually the fears receded, but years later Jean found that her mother's advice was helpful in her writing as well as in her family life. She learned to take the exciting ideas her imagination presented to her and shape them so that her stories said something enlightening to her readers.

In her book *Kate*, Jean tells the story of a girl who goes to school, has friends, likes to read books and writes a bit of poetry. Just hearing that summary a reader might think, "I do all those things. What's so interesting about that?" But Jean, by making her imagination her servant, forced it to select, from among all the possible incidents in Kate's life, those that would create a story both interesting and challenging to the reader. So we live with Kate through the first meeting she has with a grandfather she didn't realize was still alive and watch her grow toward an understanding of some difficult choices her father had made as a young man.

Through Jean's imagination, the reader has a chance to step into Kate's shoes and feel what living her life is like.

# CHAPTER 7

# A *House*
*Full of Women*

In 1942, when Jean was 10, the war which had been raging in the background suddenly erupted into the Littles' peaceful family life. The Navy wanted Llew. In 1940, when he had first applied, the navy had decided that he had too many family responsibilities. Now, they were short of doctors, so Llew felt he must go. The family practice was established, and Flora could carry on by herself. But it was an upsetting time for everyone, Jean remembers.

"Hugh and I went to the station when Dad left. On the way back Mother was crying. Hugh couldn't understand what was wrong and kept saying, 'Why are you crying?' I remember kicking him to make him shut up because I understood a little more than he did."

Even so, Jean was too young to understand the danger to her father. The war was too remote. Although they heard radio broadcasts and her mother worried about torpedoes when her father was at sea and buzz bombs when he was in London, there was no television to help Jean picture where her father had gone or what he was doing.

"I knew just enough to figure out there was something to worry about but not enough to believe anything could go wrong."

To children living in small Canadian towns, the war meant girls singing "Till the Lights of London Shine Again," Princess Elizabeth on the radio rallying the children of the Empire to the war cause, war evacuees staying with Canadian relatives to keep them safe from the bombs falling on Britain, expeditions to gather milkweed pods (the silk was used to stuff life preservers), and giving up allowance money each week to buy war-savings stamps.

Each 25-cent stamp was stuck on a card issued by the government. Four dollars worth of stamps filled the card. The government promised that seven and a half years later you could redeem your four-dollar certificate for five dollars. In this way, even children could loan the government money to help pay for the food, uniforms, and equipment soldiers needed to fight the war.

"I thought I'd get it back. The ads kept telling us what a lot of money we would have saved by the end of the war if we bought stamps. Quite a while after the war, I remembered the stamps. I asked Dad where my money was and he said he'd traded the certificates in long ago and bought me a winter coat. I felt so disgusted to learn that my money had been used for a coat."

During the war, many Canadian children grew up in homes full of women. The Little children were no different except that they had a mother with an office instead of a mother who did housework all day. That didn't bother Jean, though. She knew if she went to the office door and knocked, her mother would desert the patient to come and see what she wanted.

"I decided I was in favour of 'working mothers'," Jean remembers. "I noticed that the other kind never seemed to stop working, while, if we could entice ours away on a picnic or for a walk in the woods, she became completely ours and didn't fuss about all the things she had left undone — such as dusting."

But Jean also appreciated the "Doctor Flora" side of her mother especially her telephone advice to worried patients. "A sneeze is a baby's way of blowing its nose," the doctor would tell frightened new mothers. To people who gasped dramatically, "Oh, doctor, I can't breathe!" she might reply tersely, "Try stopping." She thought helping a baby into the world was the most joyous occasion in a doctor's life and she loved going off to such "birthday parties." She always felt compassion for anyone in trouble and Jean never knew when she would come home to find a needy person visiting for a day or two.

During the war years, Doctor Flora ran the family medical practice by herself. Grandma Gauld, who was living with them by then, helped look after the children. Sometimes Aunt Gretta was with them as well. All through these years, the family had a series of girls who lived in during the week and helped with the work. They were young girls just out of high school. Occasionally, they became good friends of the Littles. At times, Jean resented them.

"It was an ambivalent relationship. We made work for them, so sometimes they were annoyed with us, but we were young and they were young so they half played with us, too.

"I remember once a very special visitor was coming, a missionary, I think, and Jeanette, the girl we had at that time, said she'd make us our own little tea party if we'd really clean up our room. So we pushed everything under the bed and pulled the bedspread right down over it. It looked so beautiful. She made the tea party, brought it up to the bedroom, and sat down with us. But she sat on a low hassock which meant she could look under the bed and see the mess. Then she started to cry. It was terrible. We didn't realize we'd done anything wrong until we saw how we'd hurt her feelings.''

The children were never in any doubt when they hurt Grandma Gauld's feelings. She had a sharp tongue which she used to make them aware of each one of their faults. Grandma Gauld had lived with them ever since they had moved to Guelph. Now that Llew was away and her daughter, Flora, was often out making house calls, Grandma felt she was in charge of the children. If they misbehaved, she would lecture them about setting good examples for other children because they were the doctors' children. If that failed, she would warn them that they were breaking their mother's heart. She loved her grandchildren but as the children grew older she became more and more short-tempered with them.

''I remember one time when I was sitting out on the verandah reading. Pat, who was then three or four, knocked the potted plants off the railing with a stick. I just kept on reading. Grandma came out, found the smashed plants and turned on me. 'But I didn't do anything. Patsy did it,' I protested. That made Grandma even more furious. 'How can you blame her? She's just a baby!' I knew Patsy had done it deliberately, so I felt very abused.

''Hugh and I were at the age when we would question or talk back. Grandma would get very angry, very fierce. Once I did something she didn't like and she told me to apologize to the maid. I didn't want to. She took me by the hand and squeezed my knuckles—this was something she often did to punish us—and said, 'You apologize right now.' So finally, in frustration, I said, 'All right, I apologize.' Then I ran out the back door shouting, 'But I'm *not* sorry!'

"When we made Grandma angry, she would say to Hugh and me, 'I'm going to pack my suitcase and start down the London Road because you children don't love me.' Then she'd go to start packing and Hugh and I would follow her saying how sorry we were, but we were thinking, Wouldn't it be nice if she really did go?"

Flora was often caught in the middle of this tug-of-war. Because she was a working mother, she needed someone as concerned and caring as Grandma Gauld to help look after her children but she didn't agree with some of her mother's more old-fashioned ideas. One Saturday afternoon Jean and Hugh wanted to go to the movies to see *Bambi*. Grandma Gauld said, "Certainly not. Nice children don't go to the movies. Your mother wouldn't approve." Just then, Flora returned from a morning at the hospital. Jean challenged her immediately.

"Of course you can go," Flora replied, ignoring both Grandma's disapproving sniff and the triumph in Jean's face.

In 1945, when Jean's father returned from the war, more friction developed. He and Grandma Gauld didn't always see eye to eye. She was a strict teetotaller. Llew didn't drink but he wasn't rigid about it. To tease her, he taught Jean to sing:

> Go see what the boys in the back room will have
> And tell them I'm having the same
> Go see what the boys in the back room will have
> And bring me the poison they name.

"Grandma would pound the table shouting, 'Whiskey' — BANG with her hand — 'is the devil' — BANG — 'in solution' — BANG. It was years before I realized what that meant. I thought it was just something Grandma said when Dad teased her."

Grandma Gauld's strong personality created tensions in the Little household. Once, when she had been more than usually bullying, Jean thought of running away. But there were other compensations, one of which was the joy Jean got from the hours and hours her grandmother spent reading aloud.

She was a very dramatic reader and every night at bedtime she would bring to life *Green Gables*, *Avonlea*, *Windy Poplars*, whichever of the "Anne" books she was currently reading to the children. She went through all eight of the "Anne" series and many other books in these nightly sessions, much to the delight of Jean, Hugh, and Pat.

"Grandma was a very interesting person and, although as a child I didn't get along with her, I came to love her very much. Now I realize how difficult it was for her to cope with children as she got older. I valued her more when I became an adult."

Grandma Gauld lived with the Littles until 1960 when she died at the age of ninety-three. She is one of the reasons Jean finds it easy to write about old people and to show the adjustment problems every family member has when a grandparent comes to stay. Meg Copeland in *Spring Begins In March* fiercely resents having to give up her room when her widowed grandmother comes to live with them, but she learns, as Jean did, to become more understanding of older people and to love them for who they are.

# C H A P T E R 8

## *Friends
At Last*

$F$or Jean's first eleven years, her best friends were her brothers and sister, and her happiest moments were at home with her family. She rarely had a friend who walked with her to and from school. In fact, her main concern was to walk home in peace, free from name-calling, jibes, and taunts. Her mother, worried about this lack of friends, tried to help.

One attempt was summer camp. Surely the closeness of a group that lived, worked, and played together for ten days would give Jean a good chance to make friends her own age. Off she went to a private camp full of hope that here she would find that special friend for whom she had been searching. But she soon found that the girls at that camp weren't looking for closeness. Many of them came from broken homes. They were unhappy and cynical. One girl even slept with a knife under her pillow. Jean hated camp, but, when Flora came to pick her up, she didn't want to hurt her mother's feelings, so she sang the songs she'd learned, told about the canoe tests she'd passed, and forgot about the rest.

The next year, she was horrified to discover she'd been enrolled again "because she'd liked it so well"! Of course no one believed her when she said she'd

(Jean Little Collection)
*Jean in her CGIT middy*

hated it. Back she had to go for a second summer, resigned but determined that she would never return.

The hunt for friends was not going well but Flora had another plan in mind. That September, when Jean came home from camp and started into Grade 7, she was old enough to join CGIT. Canadian Girls In Training was a mid-week church group, a club where girls between twelve and seventeen could work out, in practical ways, the principles they discussed in church on

Sunday. Church was an important part of the Littles' family life. Jean had attended Sunday School since she was very young, but a mid-week group was different. She was sure that CGIT would be just like school with her on the outside looking in, and she didn't want to risk being rejected again.

Flora understood her daughter's fears but, much as she sympathized with them, she knew Jean couldn't be allowed to retreat into a shell. Flora had attended the first CGIT camp ever held, when she was living with her aunt and uncle in Regina, Saskatchewan. She wanted Jean to feel the warmth and companionship that comes from girls working together toward a common goal. So she insisted that Jean join.

"It was a nice warm evening in September," Jean recalls. "I was scared of going so I just dawdled and dawdled. When I arrived, they were dancing a Virginia Reel. The minister's daughter — she must have been seventeen, one of the 'big girls' I looked up to — came right over and asked me if I would be her partner. She was a very popular girl and so I was thrilled. Instead of leaving me standing there, on the edge, she made me feel at home right away."

Jean felt "at home" for a number of reasons. Activities she was good at — singing, poetry, playacting — were emphasized in this group. The leaders didn't insist she play games or do crafts in which her poor sight would hamper her. And the girls were friendly. In this atmosphere, Jean was able to relax and be her real self. And her real self, the girls soon discovered, was a very amusing person. Jean was the first to laugh at the difficulties her handicap created. This gave the other girls a chance to see behind the peculiar eyes and get to know the real Jean, a person the name-calling children in the schoolyard had never known.

(Jean Little Collection)
*Jean at CGIT Camp Council with two friends*

One girl, in particular, was delighted to find Jean at CGIT. Grace Alexander lived on a farm outside Guelph. In those years, school buses did not collect students each morning at the end of their farm lanes and deliver them to the district high school. To attend collegiate, farm children had to board in town. When Grace came into Guelph to board with her cousin Ruby, she joined the CGIT group at Chalmers United and met Jean. Soon Grace became the special friend Jean had hoped for all her school years, but not the only friend Jean had now.

The friends Jean made in CGIT carried over into school friendships. Rarely did she have the feeling of being on the outside — being considered peculiar and, therefore unlikeable.

From those years come many warm, humorous memories: performing in a mock wedding, the feeling of closeness within the group at the end of each meeting when all the girls joined hands in a big circle to sing "Day is Done", the embarrassment during a Candle-lighting Ceremony when Jean realized that the singed smell was from her smoking bangs, and the wonderful summer camps she went to every year until she was twenty-one.

Much to Jean's delight, CGIT camp was nothing like the private camp. Her church leaders were among the camp counsellors and some of her friends were there. Although she was a little homesick the first night, she loved every minute of the days. Several of her earliest poems tell about her love for the camp at Miramichi, especially the overnight hikes.

> A chilly night, some trees on guard,
> A campfire glow not far;
> Someone to share my blankets, and
> The light of a watching star.

> Sticks and stones dig into my back,
> Mosquitoes zoom through space.
> That big one with the baritone voice
> Is having a feast on my face.

Jean's experiences in CGIT and CGIT camp had finally broken through the years of reserve and loneliness that she had felt outside her family. Now she had friends who were her own age. But she soon discovered that the idealized view of friendship she had found in books wasn't always true in real life. She began to realize that the word "friend" meant different things to different people.

In Grades 8 and 9, Jean was part of a group of four girls who walked to school together. One of the four was older, prettier, and popular with boys. She liked to manipulate the group by choosing to walk with one girl one day and another the next day. Jean remembers the tension within that little group, and the feeling of failure when she wasn't chosen as the favourite. It wasn't until much later that she realized her so-called "friend" was using her popularity as a means of exercising power. The experience was useful, though, when Jean came to write *One To Grow On*. In that book, Janie Chisholm is manipulated by Lisa in much the same way Jean and the other two girls were manipulated.

Years later Jean observed:

> A friendship is a fragile thing
> — Like the dust of bloom on a butterfly's wing.
> Presuming on it is like trying
> To keep a butterfly from flying. . .

But like the Monarch Butterfly who struggles against mighty odds to migrate south:

> . . . Although it is a fragile thing
> It has the courage to take wing,
> Dare to ride the dark, and come
> Bravely home.

# "Poems Come Like Birds"

Poetry was an important part of school life when Jean was young. It was read, studied, and memorized — but *never* written.

"I'd never heard of a *child* writing a poem," Jean says.

One day, however, just before she turned twelve, Jean discovered what a useful talent writing verse could be.

"My father was reading the paper. I wanted him to pay some attention to me, so I offered to sing a song for him. He ignored me. He wouldn't even emerge from behind the paper. I said I'd do a dance I'd learned at school. I don't know why I said that because I was physically clumsy. However, he wasn't interested in that either, so I went away.

"It was a December afternoon, just at sunset. For some reason I decided to write a poem. I'd never written one before but I liked the look of the sky. Some words came to me. I wrote it in no time and went back to my father.

" 'Dad, I've written a poem,' I said, with no hope at all that he'd be interested. Well, he dropped the paper so fast that the pages flew apart. 'A poem! Let's see it.'

'' 'Boy,' I thought, 'this is the way to get attention.' And I've never stopped writing poems from that day to this.''

Jean's father was pleased that she was showing writing talent. As a young man he himself had enjoyed writing. From the time he was fifteen until he started university, he wrote, under the pseudonym Terence O'Toole, to editors of newspapers and magazines stating his opinion on articles and stories they had printed. To see his daughter following in his footsteps delighted him.

"Even so, one of the first things he wanted me to do with the poem was change it. To describe the way the clouds looked to me I'd written:

Orange flags are flying.

"He said that sounded like an Orangeman's Parade. I said, 'But they looked like flags!' I know now that I was right about the image but he was right too. The image of 'flags' shouldn't have been in the first line. I should have set the scene so the reader would know I was comparing clouds to flags. But he didn't quite realize what was wrong and I didn't believe he was right.''

The year Jean turned fifteen her father had thirty of her poems printed in a small book. Before the manuscript went to the typesetter he changed the line that had so irritated him. Now Jean's first poem begins:

Orange clouds were drifting
No overhanging grey
Dimmed the rosy sunset
At the close of day.

Llew called the book *It's a Wonderful World*. He had an artist friend illustrate some of the poems and a printer in Guelph produce it. When the book was displayed in local bookstores, it sold briskly.

Jean was delighted and began to make plans. ''I thought it was going to be great to have all that money, but Dad donated it, in my name, to Camp Miramichi. The money was used to build a fireplace. I was sort of torn between being proud and wanting that money myself.''

When Jean entered high school, her writing was encouraged by an understanding English teacher, Isobel Cowie.

''I remember once we had a page of questions we were supposed to answer about *Romeo and Juliet*. Instead of answering them I handed in a great outburst on my feelings for the play. Some teachers would have said, 'This is all very well but you didn't answer the questions.' Miss Cowie wasn't like that.

''After I read Scott's *The Lady of the Lake* I wrote a poem about it and she accepted that as my book report. She was willing to bend the rules.

''Many years later, I met a friend from school days who said he could remember her reading to his class things that I had written and saying this was what every pupil should be doing.

''English was the only class where I could shine so I always had my hand up, but Miss Cowie would never ask me the easy questions. I hated that, but I realize now it was really a compliment that she saved the more difficult ones for me.

''The year I was in her Grade 10 class, I got 98 on an exam. She said she'd never given over 95. I'd made one grammatical error. I said: Everyone took their lunch. She lopped off two marks. I've never made that error since.

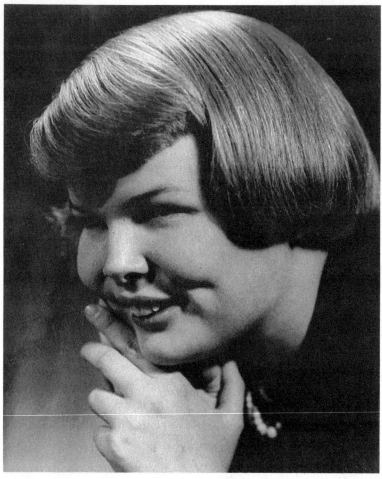

(Jean Little Collection)
*Jean at 17*

"I won an anonymously donated prize that year, for the highest English marks in the school. I have since thought that Isobel donated that prize. I was failing in everything but English and history. It was a great boost for me to get up in the Assembly to receive a prize."

In a burst of affection for her English teacher, Jean named one of her goldfish "Miss Cowie."

Poetry writing had become a permanent part of Jean's life by the time she was in high school. She found it was a satisfactory way of sorting out her thoughts and one sure way she knew she could receive recognition.

Twice more in her teenage years she had success with her writing. When she was in Grade 13, she entered a contest for which she had to write an essay called "Our Way To Peace." The prize was a trip to England — no small incentive for someone who loved English literature and wanted to visit the homes of her favourite authors.

"I wrote an essay suggesting that the whole world should learn Esperanto (a 'universal language'). There were three judges and I got a letter from one saying that although somebody else had been given the prize, my writing was better. He said I should certainly pursue writing."

Something even more exciting happened when Jean was seventeen. She wrote two poems, one called "Mary," the other "Joseph." They told of the thoughts Mary and Joseph might have had as they travelled the long road to Bethlehem just before the birth of Jesus. Her father sent the poems to the editor of *Saturday Night* magazine which, to Jean's astonishment, accepted them. Just before Christmas, the poems appeared at the front of the "Women's Section," set out on a full page with black borders around them.

A week after the poems were printed, a letter appeared in the "Letters To the Editor" column. A man in Oakville had written to praise the poems and ask the editor to make sure his reading public heard more from this talented, young writer.

Jean first heard this news on her way to school. Someone asked her, "Did you see the letter?" At school, all the teachers were talking about it.

Jean was ecstatic. She raced into the house at lunch-time screaming, "Mother, Mother, someone wrote to *Saturday Night*. He said he wanted to know more about me!"

Flora turned to confront her husband. "You didn't!"

"Why not?" he answered with a grin. Then Jean realized that her father had been the correspondent. He had signed the letter with a fake name and mailed it one day when he was out of town.

"I was mortified," Jean remembers. "When I went back to school in the afternoon, everyone was talking about the letter and I couldn't tell them my father had written it. It was years before I realized what a loving thing it was for him to do."

The mortification was soon replaced by a thrill. A cheque for thirty dollars came from the editor of *Saturday Night*. "I thought it was a bill. I'd never seen a cheque made out to me. But I had fun deciding how to spend it. I made lists of things I could buy for thirty dollars. A Great Dane puppy, I remember, headed one list. Then my mother suggested I use the money to buy material for a dress for the school formal. So I bought thirty dollars worth of emerald green French velvet."

Is writing poetry easy or difficult? Years after her high school days, when Jean was the author of ten novels and hundreds of poems, she wrote a short story in which the main character scribbles poetry when she should be doing arithmetic homework. In the story, the girl, Janet, writes a poem that sums up Jean's own feelings about how poetry happens:

Poems come like birds.
When you call them, they stay away
But if you sit very still
And pretend not to notice
One might fly to your shoulder.

# C H A P T E R 10

## *Special Friends*

Jean excelled in English class and was managing in History but she had great difficulty with other subjects. She could not focus a microscope, do map work, observe the results of a chemistry experiment, or dissect a frog. She had enough sight to sketch — an activity in which she delighted — and enough to read — which was an enduring pleasure — but the academic side of high school was mostly a source of frustration and failure for her.

The social side, however, was more satisfying. CGIT had given Jean friends like Grace Alexander. These friendships had carried over into school so that she no longer felt as much an outsider — different and therefore to be ignored. Because she was happy, she relaxed and learned to be more outgoing. This, in turn, attracted others to her and started a happier life than the one she had been caught up in during her elementary school years.

Jean and Grace walked to school together, did homework together, and spent innumerable hours in Jean's bedroom at the top of the big house on Queen Street, talking about life, their futures, and, of course, boys. But although boys in general were an interesting topic of conversation, boys in particular didn't have much place in the girls' lives yet. Jean had no boyfriends in high school. She was still unsophisticated enough to feel awkward around boys.

In Grade 10, Jean was invited to a mixed party. She was about to turn down the invitation when her mother said, "Of course you'll go. It's lovely you were asked." And she refused to listen to any of Jean's excuses, thinking it a good opportunity for Jean to get out and mingle with people her own age.

Jean was miserable. She felt too embarrassed to tell her mother that she was sure it was going to be a "necking" party. She knew she would have only two choices —join in or stand on the sidelines showing disapproval. She couldn't see how she could do either.

Just before the party, however, Jean fell and broke her ankle. Flora expected sulks and restless boredom when she prescribed three weeks in bed, but Jean was delighted. She'd been saved from the party!

With so much quiet time on her hands, Jean found story ideas popping into her head. To amuse herself she started to write a long story which turned into a novel in the form of a diary.

"I remember Mother saying, in astonishment, as I sat in bed scribbling away at my story, 'You're the perfect patient,' and I thought, 'If only you knew . . . !'"

Jean's reluctance to go to mixed parties was not unusual in the forties. Some girls had "steadies" but many were still happy to have hikes, picnics or parties with girls only. It was a relaxing time to grow up without excessive pressures of being paired off.

Grace was Jean's closest friend through these years. Even though Grace wasn't particularly interested in books, Jean felt comfortable with her. They were kindred spirits, the very thing for which Jean had always longed. They walked home from school together avidly discussing the day's events and often met in the evening for homework sessions or a trip to the movies.

One evening, Jean and Grace were coming home from a movie called *I Wake Up Screaming*. They arrived at Grace's house and, as usual, stood talking by the gatepost for a few minutes. Finally, Jean decided she had to go home.

"Be careful," Grace warned her as they stood looking down the dark street.

"I'll phone," Jean promised, "if I'm attacked on the way home."

As she hurried along the dimly lit streets, Jean was thinking about her old bugbear, the kidnappers. What a relief it was to reach the safety of her front hallway! Just inside the hall door, an impish thought struck her. She ran to the telephone and dialled Grace's number.

"Grace . . . " she whispered into the mouthpiece, "I've been kidnapped. I'm tied to a chair . . ."

"Wait!" Grace shrieked. "I'll get Ruby."

"She took it seriously," Jean remembers ruefully. "She didn't stop to question how I could phone if I was tied up. My laughter finally convinced her it was a joke."

But Jean was amply paid back for that joke on another evening when she was coming home alone from a theatre performance.

As Jean passed the house she had always thought of as "The Kidnapper's House" a man came out. He went down the path and turned onto the sidewalk behind Jean. Her heart began to pound. Quickly she turned the corner. He turned the corner. She started walking faster. He started walking faster! What more proof did she need? He *was* a kidnapper. In desperation she spun round to confront him and realized he was taking a handkerchief from his pocket. "For the gag!" she thought, remembering Jamie's story. Clenching her fist she hit him as hard as she could. Minutes later she ran into her house sobbing hysterically.

"What happened to you?" her father demanded.

"There was this kidnapper . . ." she gasped and told them the story.

Llew gave a roar of laughter. "Poor man," he said. "He's walking along, minding his own business and decides to blow his nose. The next thing he knows he gets a great wallop on the head."

"I could see it was funny," Jean remembers, "but even so I was terrified. I suppose Jamie hadn't even made the story all that scary. It just grew bigger and bigger in my mind."

For most of Jean's high school years, the Littles lived in a big house on Queen Street which Jean was to use later as the setting for *Look Through My Window*. This house gave the family room to breath, places for growing children to have privacy, and a big yard for playing. It also gave them room for pets. Jean had always wanted the kind of pets that children had in books, a Lassie or a Black Beauty or a Greyfriars Bobby. She wanted a pet that would follow her around, sleep on her bed, and, most important of all, love her best.

Life, however, seldom is as accommodating as fiction. When Jean was fourteen her aunt bought her a pup from the local farmer's market.

"Skippy was a nice little pup but he had feet like snowshoes and grew up to be the size of a collie. The first day we brought him home from the market, Hugh and Pat wanted to feed him and take him for walks. I wouldn't let them. Skippy was to be my dog. Of course, by the fourth day I was tired of taking him for walks so I said they could. But the novelty had worn off. They didn't want to walk or feed him. That dog turned out to be a bit of a disaster. We didn't have a fenced-in yard, so he was always running away.''

Cats presented different problems. Jean had only one cat — a tiger-striped one she named William Shakespeare.

''I think he was part of a litter a friend's cat had. I remember seeing the kittens born, the only animals I've ever seen born. They came in little transparent sacks like Saran Wrap. That picture stayed with me so vividly that I used it in *Look Through My Window*. I think I wanted this cat because of all the cats Anne Shirley in *Anne of Green Gables* was so emotionally attached to. I liked William but I don't think he liked me, either because I would be very loving one day and then pay no attention to him for ages, or perhaps because he was attached to places more than people.''

When the Littles moved from Queen Street to Woolwich Street, their yard was too small for a dog that was used to running free. One night, Skippy refused to come when Flora called him. Llew had had enough. The next day, Jean arrived home from school to find both dog and cat gone to the Humane Society.

''I cried so hard they took me to get William Shakespeare back, but when we moved to the new house, that silly cat wouldn't stay. Four times he crossed the city to the old house and yowled outside, wanting to be let in. Eventually even I could see he had to go. Dad made me take him to the Humane Society on the theory that if I was part of making the decision I wouldn't blame him later.

''I like cats but I like dogs better. Dogs come when they're called, which is easier if you don't see well. I guess you start off having dogs *or* cats and you stick with it. That's what I've done.''

The names Jean chose for her pets often reflected her current interests. William Shakespeare was named after the famous writer. Her two goldfish were named after her favourite grown-ups, Isobel Cowie, her English teacher, and Marg McColl, her CGIT leader.

One day nine-year-old Pat decided to change the water in the fish bowl. Instead of dipping the fish out of the big bowl into the smaller one she tried to tip the water away with the fish still in the bowl. Suddenly both fish slid over the edge and, to her horror, disappeared down the kitchen drain. Slowly Pat put the bowl down and went to break the news. Bracing herself, she said,

"I've done something awful. Promise you won't be mad."

"What did you do?"

"Promise you won't be mad if I tell you."

"WHAT did you DO?"

This verbal ping pong match went on until Pat finally panicked and confessed, "I let Miss Cowie and Marg go down the drain."

Seeing the look of outrage that swept over Jean's face, Pat turned and ran. Jean came pounding after her.

"She didn't catch me," Pat remembers. "She rarely caught me in any chase. It must have been frustrating for her not to be able to keep up.

"Another time, I remember, I had been given a bike, roller skates, and a canvas hammock for my birthday. It wasn't safe for Jean to use the first two, but she loved using the hammock. One afternoon I wanted to lie in it myself. Jean wouldn't get out. I sat beside her and kept kicking the bottom. Finally Jean jumped up in a rage and chased me down the long front yard to the sidewalk. At street level she tripped on the curb and sprained her ankle. When she called for help I thought she was trying to trick me. I wouldn't go near her."

Flora let her children sort most of these problems out for themselves. Only if they took advantage of Jean's poor sight did she intervene. She understood better than they did how limited Jean's vision really was.

One August evening she and Jean had been walking along the beach. Overhead the night sky was brilliant with stars. Suddenly Jean said, "Look, Mother. There's a beautiful star in the sky." For the first time, Flora saw the world through her daughter's eyes and realized how much she missed.

Even so, she wasn't always Jean's avenging angel. The day Jean turned the hose on Pat instead of watering the garden, Flora came running out, grabbed the hose and drenched Jean. Flora believed in practical justice! Pat was delighted.

As Jean and Pat grew older, the six-year age difference dissolved. They became equals instead of older sister and younger sister, and they found ingenious ways to compensate for Jean's lack of sight so that they could do things together.

One of the best was the tandem bicycle. Jean loved the feeling of freedom bicycle riding gave her. When she was younger she would do anything to get hold of a bicycle, including paying her brothers or sister for the use of theirs. She had been forbidden to ride because she couldn't see oncoming traffic but whenever she had the chance she rode a borrowed bike around the quiet back streets. One day, she was riding happily along what she thought was the street. Suddenly she found herself wobbling onto a low verandah headed straight for a startled man who had been quietly reading his paper. After that, she left bicycles alone until she and Pat had the chance to buy a tandem bicycle.

"I remember once Pat and I were on the tandem and she complained that I wasn't pedalling hard enough. We came to an intersection where five roads crossed. Just as we reached the middle, Pat yelled, 'Pedal for your life. We're going to be killed!' Then she took her feet off the pedals. Of course I burst into activity and the bicycle shot across the intersection.

" 'I knew you weren't pedalling!' she said smugly.

"We had a lot of fun on that tandem before Pat got her driver's licence and I went away to university."

Jean's friendship with her sister became more and more important to her as the four children grew older. Hugh, who had been her childhood playmate, had his own circle of friends in high school. Jamie was nearly finished high school when Jean began. Before that, during their years in the Orient and the war years, he had been away at boarding school. Even though her brothers were no longer her playmates, they still treated her as a friend. One such occasion occurred when Jean was in Grade 13. (That was the year Jean received the cheque for thirty dollars for the two poems she had written and had a dress made up.)

"I'd never been to a formal before, so I asked Jamie, who was in college, to take me. It was quite exciting going with a college man, even if he was your brother.

"Before we went, Hugh taught me to dance. We practised up in the attic, and became quite good at waltzing. Hugh had a girlfriend who was very small. Whenever they pivotted, she would fall over his foot, so he promised me that if there was a waltz *we* would show off *our* pivot."

It was a magical occasion for Jean, but the best was saved until last. Later in the evening, there was a waltz contest. Hugh came to collect his sister for the promised dance.

(Jean Little Collection)
*Jean in her green velvet dress at the Grade 13 formal with her brother, Jamie*

"As the contest continued, more and more couples were called off the floor. Finally, we were one of three couples left. I could hear Hugh counting away under his breath as we circled the floor. Then the judges came and told us we'd won. We were the only couple doing proper ballroom dancing. The officials asked us to demonstrate. Everyone cleared off the gymnasium floor and Hugh said, 'Now, we'll pivot.' We waltzed down the floor, then we went whipping around all the way back up. We were so proud of ourselves . . .

"I used some of that evening when I wrote *Listen for the Singing*. Anna learns to dance and goes to the formal with her brother but she doesn't have as good a time as I had."

# C H A P T E R 11

# *On to University*

High school had been a good experience for Jean. Even though she had to spread her Grade 13 courses over two years to compensate for her impaired sight, they were years of satisfaction and accomplishment. Then the question loomed. What next? Could she manage university? Might she be able to teach? Llew, enthusiastic about his daughter's growing literary skill, wanted her to try writing a book. Flora said no, she thought university should be the next step. Jean was happy to have her mind made up for her in exactly the direction she wanted to go.

The Registrar of Victoria College at the University of Toronto was not encouraging. In his opinion, a person who was virtually blind could not cope with all the reading necessary in the Honours English course. It had never been done. It probably couldn't be done.

"I may fail," Jean conceded, "but I would like at least to have tried."

"Very well," said the Registrar, "but you must take it in six years. Four years would be impossible."

Jean shook her head. "Four years," she insisted.

Reluctantly, the Registrar allowed her to fill out the application forms and pay her fees.

For the first year, Jean hired readers but she found this a slow way to get through the material. She soon discovered that most of the assigned novels and poems had large enough print for her to read as she had always read, squinting along the lines of type. The difficulty came in reading the background material. These commentaries were often printed in type so small it was just a blur to her. In this predicament her father often came to her rescue. He was ill during much of Jean's first year at university and unable to give much time to his practice, but he spent many hours searching out material for Jean's assignments. Whenever she came home for the weekend he was ready with books and ideas for her.

University life was challenging and fun until one February day in Jean's second year. She had collected her mail and was reading a letter from her father as she walked back to her room. When she opened the door, she found Elizabeth Kerr sitting on the bed waiting for her. Elizabeth, who had been one of Jean's CGIT camp leaders and one of her readers during her first year, was a close family friend. She was crying as she got up to put her arms around Jean.

Jean's first thought was that something dreadful had happened in her friend's life, but it was for Jean that Elizabeth was crying. Flora had phoned to ask her to break the news that Llew had died of a heart attack. Jean was stunned. Hadn't she just been reading a letter from her father? Numbly, she packed to go home. She couldn't believe such a thing could have happened.

Her feelings of unreality persisted all through the train journey. At home, she talked calmly with the family, then mentioned an essay she was writing about Milton. Everyone was polite but not really interested. Her father would have been asking questions and suggesting sources for material. Suddenly she understood with her heart, not just her mind, that her father was not there. He would never again be there. The calm broke.

Jean turned to her writing for comfort. Her long poem ''For My Father'' begins:

Three weeks ago they told me you were dead.
My father — gone — and I had never said
How much I loved you, how each hour I cared
That somewhere in my world you safely fared.
Between us, talk of love was barbed with wit.
Love was too real for either to admit
Its truth and treat it with solemnity.
We gave our hearts deeply — and laughingly.
And so, I did not say I found in you
A dreamer who went on and dared to do,
A man who fit no pattern ever made,
A clown, a seer, a fighter undismayed
By opposition, once he claimed the cause,
A hero riddled with endearing flaws . . .

and ends:

. . . You still occupy the space
In which I walk and think and laugh and move.
Death stilled your heart. It could not touch our love.
This truth will stand undimmed through all my years,
And, even now, can check my rising tears.
You are my father still, alive in me.
Love lets me share your immortality.

Jean gathered strength from the loving support of her family and friends.

Her second year continued with only a short interruption. She had decided that readers slowed her down too much. For the rest of her studies, she read the set texts herself and wrote the essays ''off the top of her head.'' In class, she trained herself to listen carefully, taking notes only in lectures by Northrop Frye whose

(Jean Little Collection)

*Jean graduates from Victoria College, University of Toronto*

difficult concepts she needed to reread several times.

"It was the easiest four years I ever spent in school," Jean remembers.

On Graduation Day, Jean stood first in her class of thirteen at Victoria College. She grinned as the Registrar apologized for having said it was impossible. It was a day of triumph, but what was to come next?

# CHAPTER 12

# New
# Directions

Flora had always helped Jean to be as independent as her handicap would allow. She was keenly interested in her daughter's writing talent but knew it would probably be years before a writing career would support her. Jean must train for an additional job.

Not once did Jean think she might not work. In her family, being a woman and being handicapped were not seen as obstacles to a career. And, in her family, the emphasis was on having a *useful* career. The Littles gravitated to work that involved service to others. Hugh would become a rheumatologist, Pat, a nurse in a continuing care unit, and Jamie, already launched on a career with the Royal Bank of Canada, would become manager of both the Bank's programs for the Olympics and for the handicapped. As well as running a medical practice, Jean's parents had held public office. Llew had been elected alderman for the same term that Flora was elected to the Board of Education. They were active in church and volunteer work. Jean, herself, inclined the same way. She had enjoyed working as a counsellor at a camp for handicapped children. Only her difficulty in using a microscope in high school science classes convinced her that she could not be a doctor.

Just as she was trying to sort out her future, she heard about a position available in Guelph. The Rotarians had established a centre for children with motor handicaps — disabilities which made it difficult for them to co-ordinate the movements of their arms and legs. The classes would be small. Jean thought she would be able to teach under these conditions. When she asked about the position, she was told the Centre would employ her if she took a preparatory course.

Ellen Thiel, a professor from the Institute for Special Education in the University of Utah, had come to Montreal to give a two-week course in teaching disabled children. Jean went to Montreal and took the course. The American lecturer was so impressed by Jean's ability and enthusiasm that she invited Jean to Utah for a summer semester. Although Jean was nervous about going so far from home by herself, she accepted the invitation. The course gave her the confidence she needed. She returned to Guelph to organize the Centre's school which opened in January of 1956.

Jean's class was lively and imaginative, but in one area she felt frustrated. She wanted to share her love of reading with the children she taught. In particular, she wanted stories that would show them how they fitted into the larger world. She discovered few stories, however, that were about the everyday life of handi-capped children. Stories like *Heidi* in which Clara learns to walk, then pushes her wheelchair down the mountain at the end were particularly heartbreaking for the children Jean taught. They knew they would never push their wheelchairs down the mountain.

To fulfil that need for realistic stories, Jean took a year off teaching to write *Mine For Keeps*. It is a bright, matter-

(Jean Little Collection)
*Jean accepting a book and good wishes from some of her pupils
and members of the Board of the Rotary Club. She was about to
take a leave of absence to write* Mine for Keeps.

of-fact story about Sally who has cerebral palsy. Her
family helps her to fit into a normal home and school
life despite mistakes and lost tempers. Jean entered it
in the 1961 Little, Brown Book Contest for the Year's
Best Canadian Children's Book. It won the $1,000 prize.

While she was waiting to hear about the success or
failure of her manuscript, Jean returned to teaching.
Because she was conscientious and concerned about
her students, she realized that she needed more training to give them the best help she could. At the end of
the school year, she decided to apply to the teacher's

(Jean Little Collection)
*Jean with her West Highland Terrier, Susie, the star of* Mine for Keeps

college in Toronto to take a year of basic training. Despite her proven success in the classroom, her application was rejected. The verdict — a person who is virtually blind would be hampered by too many practical difficulties in the classroom. Jean's solution was to spend the summer taking teaching courses in Utah and return to her Guelph classroom in the fall.

When the Ontario Ministry of Education discovered that she was teaching without an Ontario Teachers' Certificate, she was ordered to stop. The Director of Education told her to keep teaching and arranged for an inspector to visit her classroom. The Inspector felt that her work was competent, so she was allowed to continue teaching but soon she began to have trouble with her left eye. The vision decreased and the eye became painful. The doctors diagnosed glaucoma. After three unsuccessful operations to try to save the eye, it had to be removed.

Jean did not return to teaching. *Mine For Keeps* had been published in July 1962 during the first of her operations, and she was receiving reasonable royalties. Perhaps that was a sign pointing to her future. Jean decided to follow that direction. She would try to earn her living by full-time writing.

# C H A P T E R   13

## *Success!*

Jean's decision turned out to be the right one for her. She became a full-time writer. As soon as she finished one book, she began another. She wrote quickly and tried to complete a chapter at one sitting, even though she often spent the next day revising. Because she found it difficult to mix writing and other activities, she divided her time into blocks. She saved one whole week or month for writing and used another for lectures at universities and talks to schoolchildren, which took her across Canada and the United Sates.

When Jean first began visiting schools and talking to children about her books, she didn't always know what to expect. At a Chicago book fair, she found herself in a theatre confronting five hundred black, inner city children, few of whom had actually read her books. They looked bored and restless. How could she possibly hold their attention? As the noise level mounted, she remembered a trick that mesmerized her nieces and nephews.

"I can do something Sammy Davis Junior can do," she announced, "but none of you can do." Calmly she reached up and popped out her plastic eye. There was dead silence. She held it up for the audience to see.

"Now just keep watching me," she said as she replaced it. "Sometime before I leave, I'm going to pop it out and in again. If you're not watching, you'll miss it." She had their undivided attention for the rest of the hour. When she reached the last sentence of her speech, she repeated her parlour trick.

Losing her left eye and having it replaced with a removable plastic eye had been a very upsetting event in Jean's adult life, but it turned out to have several beneficial results. One was that she no longer appeared cross-eyed. The second was that she had found a way of quieting restless classes and inadvertently of helping a child badly in need of comfort.

The child, a girl who had lost her leg to cancer, attended one of Jean's presentations. She was sitting in her wheelchair too far back for Jean to see her. On this occasion, when Jean popped her eye out and in and got the usual reaction of "Oh, yuck!", she said, "You're just jealous because you don't have any removable parts." Several weeks later, Jean received a letter from the teacher. She told her how difficult it had been for the girl in the wheelchair to accept her loss and how angry and afraid the child was about trying to fit back into school life. The teacher had insisted that the youngster come down to the auditorium to hear Jean. Now the teacher was writing to let Jean know that her humorous remark about "removable parts" had done more to help the girl accept her artificial leg than any therapy the school had been able to give. Jean might not have been able to say those words if she'd been aware of the girl's presence. It was one of the few times her poor sight has been a blessing.

During these school sessions Jean is often asked, "Where do you get your ideas?"

"From my memories," she answers, "from my imagination, from eavesdropping and from my nieces and nephews when they were growing up."

Jean has eleven nieces and nephews. Jamie's family of three grew up in Montreal; Hugh's two boys and two girls grew up in Toronto; and Pat's four children grew up in Vancouver. They are now adults, but, as children, they spent many summers with Jean and her mother at their cottage on Three Mile Lake in Muskoka.

One summer, when Pat's two youngest children, Mark and Sarah, were visiting the cottage Jean overheard a conversation in which Sarah managed to talk her reluctant brother into taking her rowing. The manipulation was so adroit that Jean remembered the conversation and later used it as the basis for the opening chapter in *Mama's Going To Buy You A Mockingbird*. The cottage was also in several chapters of *One To Grow On*.

Jean fostered a love of books and theatre in her nieces and nephews by reading to them or taking them to plays whenever they visited. Maggie, Pat's oldest daughter, attributes her own love of literature to Aunt Jean's encouragement. When Maggie was ten, she decided to write a novel of her own. The result, "Annie Andrews", was sent off for Jean's opinion with, as Maggie recalls, "high hopes of instant publication." Jean wrote back a long appraisal saying how much she had enjoyed reading Maggie's story but holding out no hope of instant fame. (She believes in encouraging young writers but not raising impossible expectations.)

Jean was also a storytelling aunt. Her nieces and nephews were entranced by her tales but could not always separate fact from fiction. On a trip to Tallahassee, Florida, where Jean had been invited to speak to a group of teachers, she was entertaining Jamie's two boys in the back of the car while their father drove.

(Jean Little Collection)
*Jean reading to her niece, Maggie*

Suddenly young Brian asked, "Aunt Jean, why aren't you married?"

"What!" exclaimed Jean. "Why, I've been married five times." Then she began to tell the boys what had happened to each husband. The first one was a big-game hunter who had gone to Africa and been eaten by a lion. The second was a tight-rope walker who had fallen from his high wire in the circus. On she rattled, with the boys staring at her transfixed.

"And my last husband was Mr. Wessenger," Jean concluded. "He was called Wessenger the Messenger because he went all over the world with messages. One day he went to the North Pole with a message and I've never heard from him since, so you see I can't get married again until I know what's happened to him."

*Jean and Flora in Taiwan during their world tour in 1965*

(Jean Little Collection)

The boys soon caught on to the tall tale, but their little sister, Robin, believed it. One day, when she was in Grade 1, she took Jean's latest book for "Show and Tell." "My Aunt Jean wrote this book," she told the class. "And did you know she's been married five times?" Robin was not amused when her parents told her it was all a joke. The next time she saw Jean she gave her aunt an angry scolding.

Several years later when Jamie's family were visiting Guelph, the grownups sitting in the living room heard a series of strange thumps and bumps from the bedroom overhead. Jamie went up to investigate. He found Brian swaying back and forth on Chris's shoulders trying to button up a coat over both of them to make a tall man. They were practising an entrance to confront their Aunt Jean with Wessenger the Messenger, returned from the North Pole.

Jean's writing career has given her a flexible time-table which has allowed her to indulge in her love of travelling. So far, she has been in twenty-seven countries. Many of them she visited during the world trip she made with her mother.

During the British leg of that trip Jean wrote to Rosemary Sutcliffe, a writer whom she admires both for her writing and for the way she has coped with life as the victim of Still's Disease. This is a form of juvenile arthritis which has left Rosemary crippled from childhood. Jean asked for the privilege of a visit with Rosemary at her home in Arundel.

When Jean and her companion, Carol, arrived Rosemary took them out to the garden. Since they were all strangers everyone was a little tense. Jean, trying to appear at ease, leaned on the canvas back of her garden chair. The canvas tore and Jean fell backwards. To her great embarrassment she found herself wedged in the frame of the chair.

Rosemary, of course, could not help her and Carol was laughing too hard. Twisting and turning, Jean was finally able to crawl out through the back of the chair. That broke the ice. Jean and Rosemary have been good friends ever since. Jean has been back to visit at Arundel twice and maintains a steady correspondence with Rosemary.

In 1972, a friend of Jean's took a job teaching English as a second language in a school in Japan. Jean had not lived in a second culture since her seventh year. This seemed a perfect opportunity to refresh her childhood memories of the Orient. She went along for the adventure but she also wrote *Stand In The Wind* during part of the two and a half years she was in Kanazawa.

In 1974, she won the Vicky Metcalf Award for Canadian Juvenile Books. Because Jean was still in Japan, Flora accepted the prize for her daughter at the Canadian Authors Association's annual conference. It was a proud moment for her. The daughter she and her husband had nurtured in such loving and practical ways was now receiving recognition in Canada for her writing.

It is not hard to imagine how much more difficult life would have been for Jean without the constant support and love of her mother. Through Jean's adult years as well as her growing-up years, Dr. Flora Little has always been there to share her own strengths, humour, and good sense with her daughter. When Flora was voted Guelph's Citizen of the Year, Jean (who was in Japan at the time) was asked to write a testimonial. She recounted many anecdotes about her mother, including the time the family was seated at the dining room table waiting for grace to be said. Instead of "Dear Lord," Flora began "Dr. Little speaking." But Jean ended the testimonial on a serious note. "As long as she keeps things straight, however, it is all right with me if Mother retires as a doctor. Just let her try retiring from her all important position as my mother and there will be trouble. I love her enormously." It was Flora's as much as Jean's own talents that led to the string of awards now beginning to come her way.

In 1978, Jean was presented with Canada's most prestigious award for children's writing when *Listen for the Singing* won the Canada Council Prize for Children's Literature.

In the seventeen years since the publication of her first book, Jean had become a professional writer. She now had eleven books in print and at the relatively young age of forty-six should have had many productive years ahead of her. Instead she was about to go through one of the most difficult trials of her adult life.

# CHAPTER 14

# A *Writing* Life

From 1977 until 1984 no new Jean Little book appeared in stores or libraries. A story was in the making, but its unfolding was very slow. In 1978 Jean gradually became aware that the sight in her one remaining eye was blurring. The doctors again diagnosed glaucoma. No operations were attempted this time. After Jean had suffered several years of painful blisters on her cornea, the doctor decided to try a soft plastic lens to protect the eye from friction. All her life Jean had been able to read if the print was large and dark. Certainly she had been able to travel about and, most important of all, she'd been able to type her own manuscripts. Now all of these were in jeopardy.

Jean slid into depression and anger as her vision lessened and she became more dependent. She was afraid to cross streets or to walk around Guelph by herself. Then she found she could no longer see well enough to type. That could have been the end of Jean's writing career. Instead, her stubbornness and determination pulled her out of despondency. If she couldn't type, she'd find another way to "write." After months of experimenting with recorders and cassettes, she worked out a method for tape recording her manuscript drafts so that a typist could transcribe them. But the

(Jean Little Collection)

*Jean in Calgary in 1985 accepting the Canadian Library Association Medal for* Mama's Going To Buy You A Mockingbird. *Her sister, Pat, is seated at right.*

constant editing that writers find essential to produce a good book was difficult.

"When I edited, I'd use two tape recorders. I'd have to listen to my tape on the first one to see what I wanted to change, then record from one machine to the other to that point, make the change and carry on from there. It helped a bit when I learned to use a patch cord, but only if the changes were not major — just small additions or deletions. It was very frustrating, especially by the fourth and fifth drafts when the manuscript was quite long. It took me seven years to do *Mama* that way."

As the manuscript for *Mama's Going To Buy You A Mockingbird* took its final shape, Jean realized that she had to get back out into the world. Hesitantly, not sure if she could cope with this next step, she applied to a training school for a seeing-eye dog.

Seeing-eye dogs are highly intelligent and very well trained but they cannot do their work properly if their human partners are not also well trained. Jean liked dogs. She wasn't worried about sharing her life with one. She was worried, however, about letting the partnership down, not measuring up to the mobility standards set by the Seeing Eye School.

As soon as she met Zephyr, the golden labrador who was to be her partner, she loved him. That was hurdle number one over with. Then came three weeks of intensive training while she learned the voice and leash commands Zephyr would respond to. She also learned the most important lesson of all — to trust Zephyr, to believe he would keep her from walking into trees or off the ends of sidewalks onto busy roads.

They returned to Guelph partners, but not yet a perfect team. As with any partnership, they still needed time to learn to work smoothly together. But the important goal had been achieved. Jean was mobile again. Now when she goes out to lecture or be interviewed on radio and television, or to talk to school children about her books, Zephyr leads the way.

Zephyr has excellent manners and is so appealing that it is difficult for people not to pat and fondle him. But this is not allowed. A seeing-eye dog is a working dog who must not be distracted from the job of "watching out" for his owner. For this reason he must receive attention only from his owner. When Jean explains the reason for this rule to people, she is surprised to discover that children listen and obey much better than adults.

(Jean Little Collection)
*Jean and Zephyr at the airport ready to embark on a reading tour*

Jean was once again out in the world but she still had difficulty writing. Even though juggling tape recorders and cassettes had produced an award-winning book (*Mama* won both the 1984 Ruth Schwartz Award and the Canadian Library Association Book of the Year Medal), Jean needed a more efficient way to get her words onto paper. Then she heard about a new computer which had been designed by a blind man in Hamilton, Ontario. From his own experience David

(Jean Little Collection)
*Jean writing on SAM, her computer, and using a scanner to enlarge the words on the manuscript she is editing*

Kostyshyn knew that blind people depend on their ears and their fingers to make up for their lack of sight. Combining this knowledge with his expertise in computers, he created SAM (Synthesized Audio Microcomputer) a word processor and computer with a transisterized voice synthesizer. SAM can read back each sentence, word, or letter typed into his computer, allowing the blind operator to check for spelling mistakes or omissions. Best of all for Jean, SAM made editing manuscripts possible again.

A computer as clever as SAM is expensive — too expensive for a writer earning her living entirely from royalties. The $20,000.00 needed for SAM came from a number of sources — Jean's award money, a government grant, donations from several service clubs in Guelph, school children, friends and family. Thanks to SAM, Jean is independent again with no tape recorders or typists to slow down the creative process. The results are impressive — two new novels written, *Lost and Found* and *Different Dragons*, and a book of poems published, *Hey World, Here I Am!*

There are other signs of success as well. Over the years, Jean's books have been translated into French, Dutch, Danish, Japanese, and German. *From Anna*, Jean's best seller (140,000 copies sold internationally) has almost been overtaken by *Mama's Going To Buy You A Mockingbird*. The early books are being reissued in paperback. A short movie was made of *Home From Far* and a television special is being made of *Mama*.

With fifteen books in print and more to come, Jean Little is assured a place in Canada's literary community. But past successes don't necessarily make the future easier. A writer's life combines days of frustration with moments of joy. Did being blind make the struggle even harder for Jean? In 1974 she wrote:

> I have been complimented on the "courage" it must have taken to become a writer despite the handicap of my near-blindness. It is sad to be forced to admit this in print but courage had no part in it. When I decided to become a teacher that took courage — but I have given up teaching. I sit in my room now and write books about children and the thorny problems that beset them. I write such books because I remember how it was. I remember being a failure, being misunderstood, being untruthful, being greedy, being young . . . perhaps most of all being a coward.
>
> I am still afraid of many things — afraid of walking by myself into a crowded room, afraid of meeting strangers who will be perplexed by my peculiar eyes, afraid of making a fool of myself by talking too much, afraid of aloneness, afraid of death in its several guises. My books are meant to reach out to children and tell them, "You are not the only one, after all. Here is some-

one else just as small and scared and mixed-up as you are, and yet he or she is loved as you are, and loving, as you also are."

Children respond to that reaching out. In Guelph where she has visited many elementary classrooms, she is often recognized on the street. One day while she and her mother were out driving they met a schoolbus. Someone in the bus spotted Jean. Faces pressed against the windows. Arms waved. Voices called, "Jean! Jean! Remember us? Remember us?"

Of course she remembers them. She has filled her books with children just like them. But more than that, she had elevated disabled boys and girls to their rightful place within this group. That inclusion has become one of her unique contributions to the mainstream of Canadian literature for children.

# Appendix

**AWARDS**

1961   Little, Brown Canadian Children's Book Award
       *Mine For Keeps*

1974   Vicky Metcalf Award for a body of work
       inspirational to young people

1977   Canada Council Award for Children's Literature
       *Listen for the Singing*

1981   Deutscher Jugendliteratur Award
       *From Anna*

1985   Canadian Library Association Book of the Year
       Award
       Ruth Schwartz Children's Book Award
       *Mama's Going To Buy You A Mockingbird*

**NOVELS**

(in chronological order of first publication)

*Mine For Keeps*, 1962
*Home From Far*, 1965
*Spring Begins In March*, 1966
*Take Wing*, 1968
*One To Grow On*, 1969
*Look Through My Window*, 1970
*From Anna*, 1972
*Kate*, 1972
*Stand In The Wind*, 1975
*Listen for the Singing*, 1977
*Mama's Going To Buy You A Mockingbird*, 1984
*Lost and Found*, 1985
*Different Dragons*, 1986

**POETRY**

*When the Pie Was Opened*, 1968
*Hey World, Here I Am!*, 1986